CRAZY MATHS

BRATESH KUMAR SINGH

Copyright © Bratesh Kumar Singh
All Rights Reserved.

The Dedication for Completing this book goes to Notion Press , Mr. Chauhan Amit Sir , Mr. Brajesh Kumar Sharma Sir , Mr. Himank Varshney , Mr. Abhimanyu Singh , Mr. Mahesh Kumar , Mr. Dhirendra Kumar , Mr. Prashant Kumar Varshney , Mrs. Sarvesh Kumari , Mrs. Pooja Varshney , Mrs. Kiran Kumari

Contents

Foreword

This Book is being Writen by Mr. BRATESH KUMAR SINGH (
Author) , Mr. Abhimanyu Singh (Sub - Author) and Mr.Himank
Varshney (Sub - Author) . We wrote this book because we had
seen many Childrens fearing from Maths . Hence , We decided to
publish this Book . This is the Part - 1 of this book if you gave good
response we will also be motivated to publish the Part 2 of this Book
. We had Inroduced Basic Important Chapters of MATHS .

    - Authors

Preface

Hellow , I am Mr. Bratesh Kumar Singh the writer of this book . I Thanks my Sub - Writers for being a part of this . I want give a Specia Thanks for my motivational teachers and all my team members . I am very excited to like this book . I and my Sub - Authors wrote this book like this that you can understand this very easily in very simple Language . We also tried to explain it by giving some examples and 1 - 2 Exercises . That makes your practise 100 % .

If you like our book please give feedback to *brateshkumarsingh@gmail.com* .

- THANKU
- AUTHOR
- MR. BRATESH KUMAR SINGH

Acknowledgements

Author :- Mr. Bratesh Kumar Singh

Our Motivation :- Mr. Amit Singh Chauhan Sir and Mr. Brajesh Kumar Sharma Sir

Editor - Mr. Bratesh Kumar Singh

Our Team Members - Mr. Mahesh Kumar , Mrs. Sarvesh Kumari , Mr. Himank Varshney , Mr. Abhimanyu Singh , Mr. Prashant Kumar Varshney , Mrs. Pooja Varshney , Mr. Dhirendra Kumar , Mrs. Kiran Kumari Mr. Gaurav Sharma , Mr. Puneet Kumar

CHAPTER ONE

Linear Equation in one Variable

Linear Equation means A Equation with the variable of the highest power 1 .

Eg. - 2x + 3 = 85 , 5h - 95 = 4 , etc

Linear Equation in one variable means a single variable in one equation with the highest power 1.

Equation - A term consist of equal signs and variables .

Term - Constits of Operators and Variable .

Variable - A thing of which value is not fixed i.e the value of a Valible Varies .

Constant - A no. with a fixes value .

How to solve ?

1) 2x + 9 = 79

sol - 2x = 79 - 9

2x = 70

x = 70/2

x = 35

2) A no. Greater than 6 is equals to 10

sol - let a no. = a

A.T.Q

6 + a = 10

a = 10 - 6

a = 4

<u>Exercise - 1</u>

Solve the Equation :-

a) $5g + 5 = 56$

b) $8g + 55 = -44$

c) $8x + 11 = 22$

d) $2h + 55 = 22$

e) $7n + 88 = 9$

State True or False :-

1) Highest power of a linear equation is 5 .

2) Variables has a fixed value .

3) constants has a fixes value .

4) Equation consists of variable .

5) Variable consits of Equation .

Mixed Questions :-

1. Solve $x/3 + 1/5 = x/2 - 1/4$

2. Show that $x = 4$ is a solution of the equation $x + 7 - 8x/3 = 17/6 - 5x/8$

3. Find x for the equation: $(2 + x)(7 - x)/(5 - x)(4 + x) = 1$

4. A number is such that it is as much greater than 45 as it is less than 75. Find the number.

5. Divide 40 into two parts such that $1/4^{th}$ of one part is $3/8^{th}$ of the other.

6. $x + 3x/2 = 35$. Find x.

7. A is twice old as B. Five years ago A was 3 times as old as B. Find their present ages.

8. Solve : $(x + 3)/6 + 1 = (6x - 1)/3$

9. The digits of a 2-digit number differ by 5. If the digits are interchanged and the resulting number is added to the original number, we get99. Find the original number.

10. Solve : $5x - 3 = 3x + 7$

CHAPTER TWO

Rational Numbers

Defination - Any number which can be written in the form of p/q where p and q are integers and q is not equal to zero is called a rational number.

Example-5/2,-5/6,6/7 ......and many more

Addition of rational number

To add the two rational number we have to take the l.c.m. of the denominator of rational number and divide the denominator of the rational number with the lcm and multiply the answer by numerator same do with the second number and add their answer.

For example- add 2/5 and 6/10

2/5+6/10

(lcm of 5 and 10 = 10)

(4+6)/10=10/10

Subtraction of rational number

The process of subtraction is same as as addition of rational number, first we have to take the lcm of denominator and have to divide the rational number denominator with the lcm and multiplied it by the numerator same you have to done with the second rational number but this time you have to subtract the number

For example- subtract 6/7 from 7/3

6/7 – 7/3

(lcm of 7 and 3 =21)

(18-49)/21= -31/

Multipication of rational number

To multiply the rational number you have to multiply the numerator of first rational number to the numerator of second rational number and multiply the denominator of first rational number to denominator of second rational number or you can do cross multiplication

For example – multiply 5/6 and 7/8

5/6 *7/8

35/48

Divison of rational number

To divide the rational number you have to do the reciprocal of second number and multiply the numerator of first number to the numerator of second number which is obtain by the reciprocal of second number same you have to do with denominator

For example- divide 6/7 and -9/6

6/7÷(-9/6)

6/7×(-6/9)

-36/63

Properties of rational number

<u>Closure property</u>

Closure property says that is there are there are two rational number like a/b and c/d such that b and d are not equal to zero so,a/b*c/d will always be a rational number.

For example- 3/5+4/5 = 9/5 which is also a rational number.

This property works under addition,subtraction,multiplication and division

<u>Commutative property</u>

Commutative property says that if there are two rational number like a/b and c/d then a/b+c/d=c/d+a/b.this property works under addition and multiplication

For example- 4/5+8/9 = 8/9+4/5

(36+40)/45 = (40+36)/45

76/45 = 76/45

<u>Associative property</u>

Associative property says that if there are three rational numbers where there denominator is not equal to zero then (a+b)+c will ber equal to a+(b+c)

For example- (3/2+4/2)+5/2 = 3/2+(4/2+5/2)

7/2+5/2 = 3/2+9/2

12/2 =12/2

This property works under addition and multiplication

<u>Distribuutive property</u>

This property says that if there are three rational number like a,b and c and given like a(b+c) then we can solved it like a*(b+c)

Which mean a*b+a*c

For example 6(5+2) = 6*5+6*2

6*7 = 30+12

42 = 42

<u>Additive identity</u>

The additive identity of addition is 0

For example- 5/1+0=5/1

<u>Multiplicative identity</u>

The multiplicative identity of multiplication is 1

For example-5/2*1=5/2

<u>Additive inverse</u>

in additive inverse we change the sign of rational number

for example- -5/8=5/8

<u>Multiplicative inverse</u>

In multiplicative inverse we do the reciprocal of the number but not of the sign.

For example- -3/4=-4/3

Finding a rational number between two rational number

There are many ways to find a rational numbere between two rational number .

In this book we are telling only one method for that you have to take the lcm of the denominator of the two rational number and make the denominator same and then give the rational number between them but if you were asked to give 5 rational number and the total numbere of rational number we get after lcm is only 3 then you can multiply the number you get after making the denominator same by any number

For example - find ten rational number between 2/3 and 7/8

Lcm of 3 and 8 = 24

2/3*8/8=16/24 7/8*3/3=21/24

As you can see we are able to get only 4 rational between them .so now you can multiply the these numbersb by any number

16/24*10/10=160/240 21/24*10/10=210/240

So the ten rational number are 161/240,162/240,163/240,164/240,165/240,166/240,167/240,168/240,169/240 and 170/240.

<u>Exercise</u>

Find 20 rational number between

1)23/40 and 89 /91 2)3/7 and 6/4

Do multiplicative inverse of following

1. -4/5 2)9/6

Do additive inverse of following

1)8/-9 2) 8/2

Explain each property of rational number with an example

If raju has 7/8 number of apples and give 3/2 number of apple to someone so how many apples does raju have?

Solve the following

1)8/9+(-9/8+8/9) 2) 8/7(3/9+8/7) 3) 4/5*2/3 + 4/5*9/5

CHAPTER THREE

Exponent and Power

Definition - An expression that represents repeated multiplication of the same factor is called the power.

The number 5 is called the base, and the number 2 is called the exponent.

$$5^2 \quad \textit{Example}$$

The number corresponds to the number of times the base is used as a factor.

$$(-a)^n = \{ \ a^n, \text{ when N is even } \}$$
$$= \{-a^n, \text{ when N is odd } \}$$

In this chapter, we shall be dealing with the exponent and power of rational numbers.

Positive integral exponent of a rational number .

Let ab be any rational number and N be a positive integer. Then,

$$ab^{\ n} = ab \times ab \times ab \times \ \text{N times} = a \times a \times a \times ..n \ \text{times} \, b \times b \times b \times ..n \ \text{times} =$$

anbn

Thus, $\{ab\}^n = anbn$ for every positive integer n.

Negative integral Exponent of a Rational number

Let ab be any rational number and n be a positive integer.

Then, we define, $\{ab\}^{-n} = \{ba\}^n$

Also, we define, $[ab]^0 = 1$.

EXERCISE 2A

1. Evaluate:

1. i. 4^{-3}
2. ii. $[-3]^{-4}$
3. iii. $(-23)^{-5}$
4. i. $[53]^{2} \times [53]^{2}$
5. ii. $[98]^{-3} \times [98]^{-3}$
6. iii. $[-23]^{-3} \times [-2]^{-2}$
7. iv. $[-35]^{-4} \times [-25]^{2}$
8. Evaluate: $\{[13]^{-3} - [12]^{-3}\} \div [14]^{-3}$
9. Evaluate: $\{[43]^{-1} - [14]^{-1}\}^{-1}$
10. Evaluate: $\{[5^{-1} \times 3^{-1}]^{-1} \div 6^{-1}\}$
11. By what number should $[-6]^{-1}$ be multiplied so that the product becomes 9^{-1}?
12. By what number should $\{-23\}^{-3}$ be divided so that the quotient may be $\{427\}^{-2}$?
13. If $5^{2x-1} + 25 = 125$, find the value be of x.

NUMBERS IN STANDARD FORM

A number written as $\{ m \times 10^{n} \}$ is said to be in standard form if m is a decimal number such that $1 < m < 10$ and n is either a positive or a negative integer.

1. Expressing very large numbers in standard form.
2. Expressing very small numbers in standard form.

Exercise2B

1. Write each of the following number in standard form.

i. 3500000 ii. 46300000000000 iii. 273000000000000000

2. Write each of the following number in usual form.

  i. 2.5×10^4 ii. 6.912×10^8 iii. 5.17×10^6 iv. 1.679×10^9

3. Write each of the following number in standard form.

  i. 0.00006 ii. 0.000000083 iii. 0.000000165 iv. 0.00000000689

4. i. the height of the Mount Everest is 8848 m. write it in standard form. ii . the speed of light is 30000000000 m/second. Express it in standard form. iii. The distance from the earth to the sun is 149600000000 m. write it is standard form.

CHAPTER FOUR

Interest

Interest is amount which we gave when we had taken a borrow or loan from bank or another parties . 0

Interest is of 2 types :- Simple and Compound .

<u>Introduction :-</u>

Interest - Extra money we give when we had taken a loan .

Principle - Total Money we had Borrowed ,

Time - Total period of which we had borrowed money .

Rate - At what rate you will pay interest .

Amount - Total Money you will give after borrowing moneyb . (Principle + Interest)

Profit - Amount more than the C.P

Loss - Amount Less than C.P

Cost Price - Amount in which a product is buyied ,

Sell Price - Amount in which a product selled .

Profit % - Profit in Percentage .

Loss % - Loss in Percentage .

<u>Simple Interest</u>

Simple Interest is the interest which you can find easily . It you know the Principle , Time and Rate .

eg. - Find the interest if P = 25000 , T= 1 year , R = 5%

S.I = (PTR)/100

(25000*1*5)/100

125000/100

1250 = INTEREST

<u>Compound Interest</u>

Compound Interest is the interest which increses year by year . Compound Interest is Amount - Principle .

Amount = $P(1 + R/100)^n$

P = Total money Borrowed , N - No. of years (time)

eg. - Find a Compound Interest of P = 12000 , N- 3 years , R = 5%

.

A = $12000(1 + 5/100)^3$

12000*21/10*21/10*21/10

13891.5

So, Amount = 13891.5

and C.I = 13891.5 - 12000

= 1891.5

<u>FORMULAS</u>

S.I = (PTR)/100

A = P + I

C.I = A - P

Profit % = Profit / C.P *100

Loss % = Loss / C.P *100

Profit = S.P - C.P

Loss = C,P - S.P

<u>EXERCISE</u>

1) A sum of money at simple interest amounts to Rs. 850 in 3 years and to Rs. 900 in 4years. The sum is:

2) Maninder invested into two different schemes, P and Q at simple interest rate,an amount of Rs. 15,000. Rate of interest for scheme P & Q were 14% p.a. and 18% p.a. respectively. If the total amount of simple interest earned in 2 years be Rs. 5000, what was the amount invested in Scheme P?

3) A sum of Rs. 15,000 amounts to Rs. 19,500 in 5 years at the rate of simple interest. Whatis the rate of interest?

4) How much time will it take for an amount of Rs. 900to yield Rs. 81 as interest at 2.25%per annum of simple interest?

5) A money-lender claims he lends money at simple rate of interest of 10% per annum. But he cleverly tricks the farmers by including the interest amount in the principal when he calculates

it every six months. The effective annual rate of interest he is charging is:

6) A sum of money triples itself in 12 years at simple interest. Find the rate of interest?

7) The price of a T.V. set is worth Rs. 20,000 that needs to be paid in 20 installments of Rs. 1,000 each. If the rate of interest be 6% per annum, and the 1st installment be paid at the time of purchase, then the value of the last installment covering the interest will be?
A. Rs. 17,000

8) How much Simple Interest can a person get on Rs. 8,200 at 17.5% p.a. for a period of 2 years and 6 months?

9) In what time will Rs. 4,000 lent at 3% per annum on simple interest earn as much interest as Rs. 5,000 will earn in 5 years at 4% per annum on simple interest?

10) The S.I. on a certain sum of money for 3 years at 8% per annum is half the C.I. on Rs. 4000 for 2 years at 10% per annum. The sum placed on S.I. is?

CHAPTER FIVE

Mensuration

Mensuration generally is denoted with perimeter and area we have already know about this topic in our earlier classes

<u>Perimeter</u>

Perimeter means the length of the outer boundary of a figure.

For example – find the perimeter of of a rectangular land whose length is 40cm and breadth is 20cm.

Given,

Length of rectangular land = 40cm

Breadth of rectangular land = 20cm

Perimeter = 2(l+b)

= 2(40+20)

=2*60

=120cm

Hence,perimeter of rectangular land = 120cm

<u>Area</u>

The area means the space covered by any figure

For example- find the area of a square whose side is 10cm

Given,

Side of square=10cm

Area= $(side)^2$

=10^2

=100

<u>Volume</u>

Volume means a the area occupied by a 3d figure.

For example – find the volume of a cylinder whose radius is 7cm and height is 8cm

Given, radius=7cm

Height=8cm

Volume of cylinder=$\pi r^2 h$

= 22/7 ×7^2×8

=1232cm^2

<u>Surface area</u>

Surface area is the sum of all the area of the shape.

For example – find the area of a cuboid whose length=9cm breadth=5cm and height= 24cm.

Given,

Length=9ccm

Breadth=5cm

Height=24cm

Surface area of cuboid= 2(lb+bh+hl)

=2(9+5+5+24+24+9)

=76cm^2

<u>Formulas</u>

1) Here all the formulas are listed below-

2) Perimeter of rectangle=2(l+b)

3) Area of rectangle=l×b

4) Perimeter of square= 4×side

5) Area of square=side^2

6) Area of parallelogram=base×height

7) Area of a triangle=1/2×base×height

8) Area of a trapezium-(1/2)h(a+b)

9) Arae of a rhombus- 1/2×diagonal^1×diagonal^2

10) Total surface area of a cuboid- 2(lb+bh+hl)

11) Lateral surface area of a cuboid- 2h(l+b)

12) Volume of a cuboid- lbh

13) Total surface area of a cube-6a^2

14) Lateral surface area of a cube- 4a^2

15) Volume of a cube-a^3

16) Total surface area of a cylinder- $2\pi r(r+h)$

17) Lateral surface area of a cylinder-$2\pi rh$

18) Volume of a cylinder- $\pi r^2 h$

<u>Exercise</u>

a) Find the height of a cylinder whose radius is 14cm and total surface area is 400cm^2

b) Find the length of a rectangle whose perimeter is 24 cm and breadth is 7cm

c) Find the total surface area of a cylinder whose radius is 21cm and height is 70cm

d) Find the side of a square whose area is 200cm^2

e) The area of a triangle and parralelogram is same find the base of the triangle and prralelgram if height is 24cm and area is 40cm

f) Find the surface area,total surface area,volume of cube,cuboid and cylinder if height is 24cm length is 26cm radius is 14cm .

CHAPTER SIX

Quadrilaterals

Let A, B, C, D be four points in a plane such that no three of them are collinear and the line segments AB, BC, CD and DA do not intersect except at their end points. Then, the figure formed by these four line segments is called the Quadrilaterals ABCD.

In a quadrilateral ABCD

i.   The four points A, B, C, D are called its vertices.
ii. The four line segments AB, BC, CD, and DA are called its sides.
iii. <DAB , <ABC , <BCD and <CDA are called its angles, to be denoted by <A , <B , <C and <D respectively. And ,
iv. The line segments AC and BD are called its diagonals.

Adjacent sides of a Quadrilateral

Two sides of a quadrilateral which have a common end points are called its Adjacent sides.

In the given figure ; (AB , BC) ; (BC , CD) ; (CD , DA) and (DA , AB) are four pair of adjacent sides of quadrilateral ABCD.

Opposite sides of a Quadrilateral

Two sides of a quadrilateral are called its opposite sides if they do not have a common end points.

In the given figure ; (AB , DC) and (BC , CD) are two pair of opposite sides of quadrilateral ABCD.

Adjacent Angle of a quadrilateral

Two angle of a quadrilateral having a common arm are called its adjacent angles.

In the given figure ; (<A , <B) ; (<B , <C) ; (<C , <D) and (<D , <A) are four pair of adjacent angle of quadrilateral ABCD.

Opposite Angle of a Quadrilateral

Two angle of a quadrilateral which are not adjacent angle are known as opposite angles.

In the given figure ; (<A , <C) and (<B , <D) are two pair of opposite angle of quadrilateral ABCD.

Angle Sum property of a quadrilateral

Prove that the sum of the angles of a quadrilateral is 360˙ .

PROOF Let ABCD be a quadrilateral join AC.

Clearly, <1 + <2 = <A

And, <3 + <4 = <C

We known that sum of the angles of a triangle is 180˙ .

From triangle ABD , we have

<2 + <4 + <B = 180˙.

From triangle ACD , we have <1 + <3 + <D = 180˙.

Adding the angle on either side , we get:

<2 + <4 + <B + <1 + <3 + <D = 360˙.

(<1 + <2) + <B + (<3 + <4) + <D = 360˙.

<A + <B + <C + <D = 360˙.

HENCE, the sum of the angles of a quadrilateral is 360˙.

<u>Things to remember</u>

1. If A , B , C , D are four points in a plane such that no three of them are collinear and the line segments AB , BC , CD and DA do not intersect except at their end points , the figure formed by these four line segment is called the quadrilateral.

2. The sum of the angle of a quadrilateral is 360˙ .

EXERCISE

Fill in the blanks:

  i. A quadrilateral has .... sides.

 ii. A quadrilateral has .... angles.

iii. A quadrilateral has .... vertices, no three of which are ....

.

iv. A quadrilateral has .... Diagonals.

v. A diagonal of a quadrilateral is a line segment that joins two .... Vertices of the quadrilateral.

vi. The sum of the angle of a quadrilateral is ....

Prove that the sum of the angles of a quadrilateral is 360·.

The three angle of a quadrilateral are equal and the measure of the fourth angle is 120·. find the measure of each of the equal angles.

The three angle of a quadrilateral are 76· , 54· And 108·. find the measure of the fourth angles .

The angle of a quadrilateral are in the ratio 3 : 5 : 7 : 9. Find the measure of each of these angles.

A quadrilateral has three acute angle , each measuring 75· . find the measure of the fourth angle.

Two angles of a quadrilateral measure 85· and 75· respectively. The other two angle are equal. Find the measure of each of these equal angles.